WHY We Live WHERE We Live

Written by Kira Vermond
Illustrated by Julie McLaughlin

Owl kids

For Vanessa. No matter where you lived, you were loved. — K.V.

For the most supportive family I could dream of, and Nicholas. — J.M.

Acknowledgments

I'd like to thank all the people who helped give this book life, especially my editor, John Crossingham, for his great suggestions and support. Special thanks also go out to Dana Murchison, David Carpenter (I'd move anywhere with you!), the Guelph Public Library, Amy Baskin, Theresa Ebden, Blayne Haggart, Robert Jan van Pelt, Karen Lindquist, Helen and U.J. McFarland, Quaid Morris, Teresa Pitman, Naomi Theodor, Arlando Whiterock (who knows everything there is about dinosaur tracks and living in the desert), and especially Nadia, Nathan, Maia, Zola, and Alfie. I write these books for curious kids like you!

Text © 2014 Kira Vermond
Illustrations © 2014 Julie McLaughlin

Owlkids Books acknowledges the financial support of the Canada Council for the Arts, the Ontario Arts Council, the Government of Canada through the Canada Book Fund (CBF) and the Government of Ontario through the Ontario Media Development Corporation's Book Initiative for our publishing activities.

Published in Canada by
Owlkids Books Inc.
10 Lower Spadina Avenue
Toronto, ON M5V 2Z2

Published in the United States by
Owlkids Books Inc.
1700 Fourth Street
Berkeley, CA 94710

Library and Archives Canada Cataloguing in Publication

Vermond, Kira, author
    Why we live where we live / written by Kira Vermond ; illustrated by Julie McLaughlin.

Includes index.
ISBN 978-1-77147-011-7 (bound).--ISBN 978-1-77147-081-0 (pbk.)

    1. Human settlements--Juvenile literature. 2. Human beings--Effect of environment on--Juvenile literature.
3. Human beings--Effect of climate on--Juvenile literature. I. McLaughlin, Julie, 1984-, illustrator II. Title.

GF101.V47 2014   j304.2   C2014-900389-7

Library of Congress Control Number: 2014932715

Edited by: John Crossingham and Karen Li
Designed by: Barb Kelly

Manufactured in Shen Zhen, Guang Dong, in July 2018, by Printplus Limited
Job #S180700162

B   C   D   E   F   G

Publisher of Chirp, Chickadee and OWL
www.owlkidsbooks.com

CONTENTS

Introduction

Hello. This is planet Earth. And see that little spot over there? That's where you live. But have you ever wondered why and how you got there?

Because your parents decided to buy or rent a house or apartment there, right? But why there? How did that happen? And what made living there possible? The real story behind where you live is actually full of surprising twists and turns you probably have never thought of.

Everybody adapts

When you look in the mirror, you don't see a cat, bird, or fish looking back at you. You're a human. But here's something you *do* share with all those furry, feathered, and scaled creatures: you've adapted to the place where you live. Not like other animals have, though. You don't grow extra fur to keep you warm for the winter, feathers to fly long distances, or gills to live under water. Instead, over thousands of years, we humans have adapted by finding ways to spread out and make homes all over the planet.

As humans we've adapted by using what makes us unlike any other species: our brainpower, our communication skills, and our unique ability to work together to live in all kinds of places—no matter how imperfect they are.

Big brains come in handy

In a few cases, the locations we choose give us exactly what we need to survive easily: warm weather, safe drinking water, plenty of food to eat, and the materials we need to create shelter. The problem is, there are only so many "perfect" places here on planet Earth. In fact, in many areas of the world, the settings we call home are far from ideal. They're steaming hot. Or freezing cold. Or dry as a dog bone. Maybe they're even areas exposed to earthquakes, tornadoes, tsunamis, or active volcanoes.

Why would anyone want to live in uncomfortable or dangerous places? Maybe because we've figured out how! We can live in cold climates because we pull energy from the Earth to heat our homes. We've even found ways to shift water closer to our towns and cities so we can drink it, flush it, and feed our vegetables with it. That's amazing!

Needs, wants, and "nice to haves"

Still, let's be clear here: when it comes to adapting to our environment—or making the environment adapt to our needs—we've done much more than simply create a nest or a burrow for our families to live in. That works for animals, but we want more than just a roof over our heads. That's why over time we've worked together to build towns and cities that offer speedy transportation, good schools, lots of jobs, and neighborhoods that make us feel welcome, happy, and safe. All these perks are incredibly important to people. So much so that without them, many of us would choose to pick up and move somewhere else.

Why We Live Where We Live is about how we humans have managed to evolve, or change, to live in sync with our planet, and how we mold our environment to suit our needs, big and small. But that's only part of the story. The BIG QUESTION is: What drives us to go to such lengths in the first place? Why do we bother?

So why do *you* live where you live? How is it even possible? Turn the page. You're about to find out!

Planet Perfect

Welcome to Earth, home sweet home for the past 200,000 years. But why do we all live here on Earth and not, say, the Moon, Jupiter, or some faraway planet? Because we can! Or to put it another way, because we can't live anywhere else—yet.

This planet is…just right

Remember the old story about Goldilocks and the three bears? Well, just like the girl who decided the baby bear's porridge suited her fine, planets need conditions that are just right in order for life to thrive. In other words, a planet must exist in a habitable zone—also known as a life zone or a Goldilocks zone.

Earth is one of these planets. It's…

- the right distance from our home star (the Sun), so the surface isn't too hot or too cold
- solid, not a giant ball of hydrogen, helium, or some other gas
- covered in water
- a planet with breathable atmosphere (air!). This air also comes in handy for carrying pollen from one plant to another; helping birds, insects, and planes fly; and even for talking (sound waves need air to travel)!
- shielded from the Sun's dangerous radiation by its atmosphere, something that also holds heat so we can stay comfortable most of the year
- a place with gravity (the force of attraction between objects, like the Earth and you) to keep us from lifting off into the sky

See? We live on Earth because it provides us with all the essential things humans, plants, and other animals need to exist.

Atmosphere
= the number one shield

Shooting stars are pretty, right? You wouldn't think so if one actually hit your home! Our atmosphere doesn't just shield us from ultraviolet rays—it's also the only thing between us and objects whizzing toward us from outer space. When meteors (also called shooting stars) enter our atmosphere, friction causes them to burn up. Even if some make it through, they're a lot smaller than they would have been and pack less destructive power. Without an atmosphere, Earth would be a more dangerous place to live—if we survived the blasts at all.

Are we alone out here?

The results are in: Earth is pretty special. Still, there are supposedly hundreds of billions of planets and stars in the universe. It doesn't seem possible that Earth is the only one that has the right stuff for life. Some scientists and astronomers believe there are other planets that can support simple cells and other organisms, but for now Earth is the only one we know of that has it all. Think about that the next time you look up at the dark, starry sky and wonder if someone's looking back at you.

Fact or fiction?

In 2013, using a very powerful telescope, scientists discovered three planets that could potentially support life.

FACT! The planets are called Kepler-62e, Kepler-62f, and Kepler-69c, and it's possible they're made up of land and water, just like Earth. Exciting, right? But before you consider setting off to explore, there's something you should know: they're really, really far away—at least 1,200 light-years away. Just one light-year, the distance light travels in space in one year, is nearly 6 trillion mi. (9.5 trillion km)! With the space technology we use now, settling these planets is impossible.

The Comfort Zone

Where would you rather live? Someplace cold and damp? Or warm and sunny? You would probably pick door number 2, and who could blame you? Physical comfort makes life easier and more enjoyable. Too bad much of the planet is often snowy, dry, wet, or steep — and sometimes a combination of these.

Climate plays a big part in where humans live. After all, deserts can be brutally hot, and the Arctic can be miserably cold. The earliest humans would often migrate to avoid danger or discomfort. But between 10,000 B.C. and 5,000 B.C., settlements started to form as people built homes to shelter themselves from the elements. Just as we do today, our ancestors used tools and experience to adapt to their area's climate and landscape. Although the technology we use to control our living conditions has evolved, the idea is the same.

Take homes, for example...

Live and learn

Climate and weather are two different things. **Climate** describes the typical weather of a particular location. So if a place is usually hot, we say it has a warm climate. **Weather**, however, is about what you see and feel when you poke your head outside.

Hot-climate houses are...

- built to let air circulate —doors and windows stay open
- made with thick walls to keep heat out
- sometimes built on stilts to let air flow under the floor
- painted using light colors to reflect the sun
- surrounded by trees, if possible, to create shade

Mountains, plains, and oceans

Climate isn't the only big natural force to impact where people live and why. Geography (or topography) also plays a part. For example, not many people live high in the mountains. The air is difficult to breathe, and it could be tough to lug supplies up to your house in the sky!

Oceans have a big effect on how comfortable a place is, too. Large bodies of water tend to moderate surrounding climate. Summers near a coast are a bit cooler. And coastal winters are a bit warmer.

Flat plains, like those you find in the middle of Canada or the U.S., are fantastic for growing wheat and other food. But farmers must be careful to conserve soil and moisture. Otherwise, drought can turn the whole area into a dustbowl. Not a pretty place to call home.

See?

No matter where we build our neighborhoods, there are ways to adapt to the natural world. Even so, some people still decide they would rather migrate (travel) to areas with a nicer climate. Why? Heating and cooling homes can be costly. Bundling up to stay warm can be uncomfortable. Even a tropical paradise has tropical storms.

It's easy to see why some of us decide to move on.

Cold-climate houses are...

- insulated with fiberglass, wood, cotton, straw, or plastic to keep heat in and cold out
- equipped with central heating using fire, oil, gas, or electricity
- given steep roofs to allow snow to fall off.
- made with smaller windows
- painted in dark colors to soak up the Sun's warmth

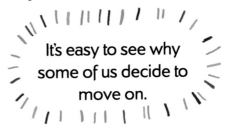

kitchen

Food in All the Right Places

Everybody needs food to survive. Good thing many areas of the world have the climate to give us what we need: fruit and vegetables to harvest, animals to hunt or raise, and fish to catch.

But what about the dry desert or cold Arctic, where there is little soil and food doesn't easily grow? You might think everybody would just pick up and move to more lush, food-friendly areas. But a lot of people choose to stay where they are because, despite hardships, they've found ways to hunt or transport food.

Follow that herd

A quick history lesson: Thousands of years ago, our ancestors lived on the move, always in search of something to eat. If a herd of gazelles was heading west, west was our new home. Our survival depended on it! Then something changed about 12,000 years ago that would have a huge effect on why we live where we do: we figured out how to grow food and raise animals to eat. Suddenly people could choose to give up their nomadic (roaming) ways to stay in one place and farm.

Would you rather eat fried bats or potato chips?

That probably depends on where you live. Although ripping into a bag of chips seems natural for someone living in North America, if you lived in Thailand or Laos, crispy, crunchy bats might be just the snack you're craving. Local tastes are formed by eating local food — even today, when we have a way of shipping new foods across great distances. Some scientists who research taste preferences believe that we like certain foods mostly because we've grown up eating what's available to us. According to them, people can learn to like almost anything. Fermented herring or puffin heart anyone?

Attention, orange and papaya shoppers...

You probably don't hunt for your next meal anymore. Instead, when many people are looking for food today, they pop down to the local grocery store or market and buy what they need. The abundance of food in many areas of the world is possible only because we've found ways to move our food closer to where we are. We've also developed farming practices that ensure more food can be grown on less land and in tougher climates. Many countries now build massive greenhouses to grow fruit and vegetables, even in the winter. And because we can ship food quickly and conveniently to wherever people reside, we can live in bigger cities or remote locations far from farmland. See what I mean...

- Oranges grow on trees in a warm southern country.

- The farmer sends boxes of freshly picked fruit to a warehouse, where they're put in crates and shipped by boat, train, or truck.

- When they arrive, they're moved to a distribution building, where storekeepers come and buy what they need to sell.

- You're with your mom or dad on a grocery trip and pick up a bag of oranges to take home.

- Lunchtime. Peel and enjoy!

Hidden costs

No local orange trees, no problem, right? Here's something to consider, though: putting food on ships, trucks, and planes uses up a lot of fuel. Because the price of oil and gas is going up, someday soon we may need to learn to live like our grandparents did as kids and eat mostly fruit and vegetables that are in season and local. Those oranges might become a luxury treat again.

Help! Not enough food

Famine — a widespread shortage of food — happens in countries that can't grow enough food for their own people and can't ship in enough from other places. Famine often goes hand in hand with drought (not enough rain), poverty, and even war. If hunger and famine strike, many families will move to other communities or even countries in search of a stable life and more food.

Just Add **Water**

Many of us take water for granted (turning on the tap, flushing the toilet…), but without water, there's no life! It's the essential molecule in the chemistry of living things, and it's something we all need to survive. Because it's so valuable, people tend to settle where the water is.

Don't believe it? Just look at a map of the world. New York, Montreal, Cape Town, Tokyo— many cities are built on ocean coasts or beside lakes and rivers. Here's why…

1 A long time ago, families looking for a place to settle down had seeds to plant and animals to feed. They wanted to find the perfect area to build shelter. Why not settle beside a river?

2 As it turns out, land in a river valley is fertile and good for growing crops. With enough extra food and water, people could stay put and raise animals. Rivers, lakes, and oceans also provided fish, still the main source of protein for up to a billion people today.

3 As time went on, people living along the banks and beaches used waterways to explore. At first, voyagers stuck close to land, but eventually some brave explorers set out into the unknown and traveled incredible distances. Major waterways became trade routes. Suddenly, people could buy interesting spices, oils, fabrics, and metals from boats docked along the waterways. Towns and cities along the water prospered.

4 Even today, water is used as a way to transport things and people, although we're now more likely to fly across the ocean than sail it. Still, some large cities have ports where ships unload everything from mangos to electronics and put them on trucks, planes, or trains to get them to a store near you.

Do we need to live near bodies of water?

Not always. There are good reasons why large communities have sprung up in places far from lakes, rivers, or oceans. Maybe the area is beautiful, close to lots of jobs, or there's family living close by. So we've found ways to twist and bend nature to meet our needs. Consider the ancient city of Petra, which sits just north of where Saudi Arabia is now. Even though it was out in the desert, historians say it collected enough fresh spring water for 100,000 people, about 12 million gal. (45 million L) a day! Citizens used a system of pools, waterways, and cisterns (big tanks).

Communities still dig wells to draw water from deep in the ground or build dams and reservoirs to store water for later. Or they build underground pipes from a source far away to move water to town. Suddenly, with a little (or a lot of) work, places that would not normally be deemed fit to live in become perfect places to call home.

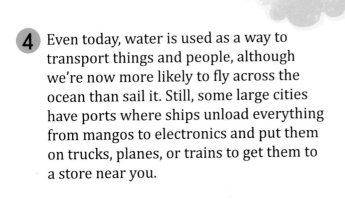

13

Power
Gives Us
a Buzz

Energy. It powers our cars, heats our homes, and keeps our TVs and computers running. Without it,electronic devices would lose their appeal...or you would move elsewhere to get the energy you want. There are scientists who believe that our need for energy touches nearly everything we do, from travel and eating to socializing and working. It is at the very core of why we live where we do today.

Energy shapes our cities and towns

Before we used fossil fuels (fuels taken from the ground) for travel, London was a long, thin snake of a city that stuck close to the banks of the River Thames. Nearly everybody lived within a half mile (less than a kilometer) of that big river and used it as a convenient way to travel. But new energy sources changed all that. Steam-powered locomotives transported people far and wide. Electricity made subways zoom underground. Oil and internal-combustion engines came together to create the first automobile. Suddenly, people could live far from where they worked, and cities spread and spread... and spread some more. Today, London is about 30 mi. (48 km) wide. The city of Atlanta, Georgia? A whopping 120 mi. (193 km)!

What's the cost?

Energy prices have an impact, too. Where gas is fairly cheap, people are more likely to drive. In regions where fuel is more expensive, towns and cities are developing ways to cut down the amount of gasoline people use. They're building more energy-efficient vehicles—and building condos downtown, where people can live and walk to their jobs.

Here are a few other ways energy shapes where we live.

1 We can live in cold climates.

With a flick of a switch or a turn of a dial, homes, schools, and workplaces in freezing winter climates turn nice and toasty. No need to head south for half the year. Why not put up your feet and stay awhile?

2 We can see after dark.

Once upon a time, people went to sleep when the Sun went down. Sure, candles gave faint light, but not enough for many activities. Having electricity means we can work, study, and play—even in places like Longyearbyen, Norway, the world's northernmost town. It experiences "polar night"—or no sunlight at all—for a few months each year.

3 We can work and make more cash.

Back when your great-grandmother was a little girl, she probably hand-washed her clothes or used an old-style washing machine. "Washing day" could take the whole day! Today, thanks to time-saving inventions like electrical washers, dryers, and vacuums, people can make money at work instead of doing chores at home. More money = more choice in where to live.

4 We can communicate.

Computers, cell phones, and landlines all run on electricity. Now we don't have to live near family to talk to them. It's possible to live in China and chat with your grandparents in France every day!

Say What?

Forget fire, the wheel, and laptop computers. Language is right up there as one of the most useful inventions we've ever come up with. We use it to share our thoughts and communicate. And humans really love to communicate! Some experts say we actually have a natural, intense drive to talk to other people. In fact, this craving for contact is one of the main reasons we make our homes where we do. Humans want to be around other people and settle down together in groups. For this to work well, we need to be able to speak our language with others — we're drawn to places where everyone speaks the same language we do.

How does language work?

Language takes an idea and matches it with a sound, and just like that, you've got a word that tells the world what you're thinking. It takes a lot of memorization, though. You have to remember that the sound C-A-R is for that thingy your mom drives. Or that I-C-H-T-H-Y-I-C means "fish-like." (You knew that, right?)

Humans typically recognize between 50,000 and 100,000 words, and can group them together to tell more complicated stories. If you say, "I'm going to school," we know what you're doing and where you're headed.

If you think about it, every time you open your mouth, a miracle comes out.

So many languages, so little brain

Only one problem with languages: there are between 6,000 and 7,000 spoken on Earth. A few of those languages are spoken by more than a billion people—others by just a handful. Either way, that's a lot of words to memorize if you want to communicate with everyone out there. An impossible number, actually. So what happens if you want to move to a part of the world where you don't speak the language? How do you communicate when you get there?

Speak to me in a way I understand

For a long time, linguists (the people who study languages) have tried to come up with ways for more people to be able to communicate with other folks around the world. You know, so that you don't have to ignore others who don't speak as you do!

Some solutions...
• Learn all the languages.
• Develop a brand-new language for everyone to learn.
• Pick a language that already exists. Have everybody study it.

The first two options don't seem to work. Most people can't learn more than four or five languages. And new languages that are planned instead of evolving naturally don't catch on. (Esperanto and Ido are examples.) So that leaves the last idea: using something that already exists.

Language really gets around

If you move to Italy, think you'll hear only Italian? Think again. There are loads of communities where non-native languages rule. In Wolverhampton, England, for instance, nearly 28 percent of people speak Punjabi. Many large cities have their own ethnic communities, such as a Chinatown or Little Italy. In these places, the non-native language is often the most common, which can attract newcomers who prefer to speak their home language — at least until they learn the new one.

Pick a language, any language

In many ways, the idea of people all learning an existing language has been put into practice for some time. Around the world, people pick English as a second language so they can talk to lots more people. If you happen to be reading this book in English, you're already on a fast track to live, study, or eventually work in many places.

There are other really popular languages, too:
• Chinese language family (1.3 billion speakers)
• Hindi (800 million)
• Arabic (530 million)
• Spanish (350 million)
• Russian (278 million)
• Urdu (180 million)
• French (175 million)
• Japanese (130 million)

These are just estimates. Researchers have a hard time pinpointing exact numbers for who speaks what. Even so, if you were to learn just these nine languages, you would be able to communicate with about 90 percent of the world! Suddenly, language wouldn't be such a barrier to living where you want.

Falling Far from the **Family Tree**

Family. You love them. You hate them. But there's no getting around the fact that your bond is STRONG. It's that connection between moms, dads, sisters, brothers, and grandparents that keeps so many families living in the same town, city, or country. Other powerful forces also come into play: money, land, work… even tradition and culture.

Live and learn

The term **nuclear family** refers to a household with only two generations: parents and children. An **extended family** is one that includes many generations: kids, parents, grandparents, aunties, cousins…

Moving on out

There are areas of the world—such as Asia and the Middle East—where it's quite common for extended families to live in one home together. And why not? There are a lot of upsides to living this way. For starters, it's cheaper to share a home. Extra people means extra help around the house, too. It can also be a lot of fun to have so many relatives around! But there are downsides. You don't get much privacy, and your home might start to feel crowded.

These customs have been changing. Kids grow up, move out, and start their own families. Grandparents live in a home on their own. Although this shift happened many decades ago in North America and some European countries, it's more of a recent occurrence in developing regions. Why does this shift happen at all?

Let's look at North America and Europe first. Many experts trace the change in living arrangements back a few hundred years to the Industrial Revolution. This revolution brought new job opportunities that were very different from life on the farm. More and more people left their families to work in factories and offices in cities. Earning more money, they could buy and rent their own homes, and even their own land.

The revolution is still going...

As technology makes jobs safer and laws ensure that kids go to school, we see this same trend happening in developing countries today. Kids get an education, land better jobs, and can buy a home for themselves when they grow up. Other changes...

Travel

In the past, travel was long, tough, and even risky. When people moved away from their families, many never saw them again. It's now possible for us to hop on a plane and travel to the other side of the world to visit family. All in one day! Can't travel? Skype and cheap long-distance phone plans make staying in touch easier than ever. Since moving away from the people you love no longer means saying good-bye forever, many are more likely to make the leap.

Expectations

If many people in your society believe that living at home is best for you and your family, you might assume that's the case, too. It's part of your culture and seems like common sense. But traditions change all the time. What used to seem like a good idea might not seem as relevant or important anymore.

Living costs more

Today, more families need two working parents to pay for all the stuff they want, not to mention the house they live in. They'll move to where the jobs are to make it happen and leave everyone else behind.

Other supports

There are daycare centers and retirement homes to care for the young and the old. Because these services are out there, grandparents no longer have to babysit their grandchildren while the parents work. So Mom and Dad—and Gramps and Gran—feel freer to move around.

Divorce

Lots of families go their separate ways when parents decide it's best that they no longer live together. If your parents have gotten a divorce, they still love you, but you might have to move somewhere new to be with one of them.

School

Someday you might decide to go to a university or college in another city or town because it has the best program or a great reputation and can lead to the job of your dreams. Smart move.

Money Is a Roam'n Numeral

Money, money, money. Everybody wants it. And for good reason. With enough access to money, your family can choose which house to buy or neighborhood to live in. On the other end of the spectrum, citizens in poor or warring countries may wish to leave entirely. But without money, there may be no way out. Here are other surprising ways in which money influences where you live.

Money doesn't make you a better or worse person. But it does give your family more options — and opportunities — when it comes time to choose a place to live.

Taxes make communities

Governments need money for roads, schools, clean drinking water, and many other services. Where do they get it? They collect money—called taxes—from citizens, residents, and businesses in their area. You can often tell whether a government collects enough taxes from its citizens and spends the money responsibly.

 A well-managed tax town has things like…

- a neighborhood pool
- safe roads
- schools with lots of after-school programs
- welcoming community centers
- parks

A mismanaged tax town has things like…

- few safe places for kids to play
- roads full of potholes
- rundown schools
- no city festivals
- no or poor garbage collection

Every country, state, province, city, or town is different in terms of how much taxation it collects and where that money goes. As you can see, taxes have a big part to play in how appealing a location is. A beautiful place with plenty of services is more likely to draw newcomers than one that can't afford those services.

Here are a few other ways money
has an impact on where you live...

Vroom!

With a car, your family can live in one place and
your parents can travel to jobs in entirely different
neighborhoods or cities. Home, work, and school
don't necessarily need to be in the same place.

Cash for companies

Some countries, like the U.S., Canada,
and India, make it easy for people to
borrow money to create businesses.
Companies need workers, so people
move to where the work is.

Easy money

Mortgages—housing loans people take out from a
bank—have been around in places like the United
States, Canada, and Great Britain for a long time. But
in other countries, they are a newer concept. Not
long ago, if you wanted to buy a house in, say, India,
you saved up for years and years until you had the
cash in hand. Now, mortgages are easier to come by,
and people around the world are borrowing money
to buy a new home today—and paying later...with
interest.

Live and learn

Interest is the money a bank charges
you to borrow money.

Immigrating for a **Better Life**

Would YOU move to another country? Many people do. It's called immigration. In Ireland in 1845, farmers dug up their potato crop, thinking they would harvest bushels of potatoes. Only it didn't happen that way. A disease had wiped out their spuds — the main food source in the country.

Over the next few years, one million Irish died during the Great Potato Famine. Another million left home for North America, England, and Scotland. Today, millions of North Americans trace their ancestors back to Ireland.

Wanted: A new life

Famine is just one factor that can push people to consider finding a new place to call home. Every year, thousands of people around the world decide they want to live in a country other than their own.

 Good reasons to move TO a new country...

- You want to go to school somewhere else.
- Your family already lives there, and you want to join them.
- You have skills that will make you money, and the new country has jobs.
- You like to explore and have adventures!

 Good reasons to move AWAY from a country...

- Your country is at war and you're scared.
- You are being threatened because of your religion or beliefs.
- You have work skills, but there are no jobs.
- You lived through a natural disaster, and your country is a mess.

What's the difference between the words "immigrate" and "emigrate"? It's subtle. Emigrate means to leave your country to live in another one. Immigrate means to come to a new country to settle.

People live where they live because countries let them in

Countries are a little like clubs. You have to belong to them in order to stay. Another word for this is citizenship. Most citizens of a country belong because they were born there. If you are a new immigrant, however, it can take years to become an official citizen. Some countries, like some clubs, are quite welcoming. They actually want more people to "join" and have policies to encourage newcomers to apply for citizenship.

 A big country needs people to fill it up.

This happened in Canada more than 100 years ago, when the government offered Europeans 160 ac. (65 ha) of free farmland in the massive country if they'd hop a (free) ship and come over. It worked. By 1910, Canada's population had doubled.

 Not enough people for jobs.

In countries where people are older and will soon retire, it makes sense to open the doors to those with job skills.

 It's about goodwill.

People in some countries make a point of welcoming immigrants because it's the right thing to do. If they can protect people who are in danger in another place, why wouldn't they?

Not everybody gets in

Just because you apply to live in another country, that doesn't mean you'll get in. Every year, governments tell thousands of hopeful people they can't come. The reasons are often political. For example, when Spain fell into economic crisis in the late 2000s, the country closed its doors to immigrants, citing money trouble and lack of jobs. In 2008, the Spanish prime minister even offered recent immigrants cash if they would leave for at least three years! But as one immigrant living in Madrid told reporters, "I came for a better life, and I got it. Food, clothing, my apartment—they're all better here than in Bolivia. I'm not interested in going back."

A History of **Cities**

Ah, country life. The cows are munching, the bees are buzzing, and all you hear is the wind. Who wouldn't want to live there? Let's take a moment to look at why people who live in small towns and the country decide to give it all up and move to the city.

Once upon a time...

On page 10, we talked about how people went from being nomadic hunters to farmers. For a long while, that was good enough. People had food, water, and shelter for their families. Then, about 6,000 years ago, a bunch of events came together that made it easier for people to live together in much bigger groups.

- Farmers discovered fertilizers and other materials to grow more food than they could eat. Storing that extra food meant feeding more people. Suddenly, some residents could become something other than farmers. They could work at jobs to help build a village or town instead.

- Societies started organizing themselves into leaders and laborers. This new social order meant everybody had a job to do, so living together became less chaotic. A well-organized community could more easily accept and provide for new inhabitants.

- People in communities from Africa to China created writing systems. Now good ideas and helpful advice could be passed down to later generations. People could spend more time coming up with new ideas to make their growing societies great!

- They created technology to make clothes, metal tools, and farm objects, which made life so much easier.

Eventually, villages grew into towns, and towns grew into cities as people developed markets, roads, waterways, and trade routes. New languages sprung up and so did religions. That didn't mean everyone moved into cities, though. Most people still lived in the country, on small farms, in villages, or in towns to be close to their friends and families. There was also still a need for farmers to feed the city-dwellers and their own families, too. In fact, even as recently as 200 years ago, only three people out of a hundred called a city their home.

Enter the Industrial Revolution

Once factories started popping up in Europe in the 1700s and into the 1800s, life took a turn and families began to leave the country looking for work. Why did they move? Some thought there were already too many people clogging up the countryside. Too many farmers meant not enough usable land to make a decent profit. Others were tired of changing weather and failing crops. Life in the city seemed a lot more stable.

But cities had problems of their own

In fact, these cities could be horrible! They smelled, since people dumped their garbage and waste out on the street, or even into their basements. All that sewage leached into the soil. Diseases tore through neighborhoods, and people died of cholera when they drank contaminated (infected and dirty) water. And those jobs? They were often just as exhausting—and nearly as low-paying—as the ones left behind on the farm.

For a while, urban areas stopped growing quickly, as they were overcrowded and many people got sick and even died. The city didn't look like a land of golden opportunity anymore—its popularity took a nosedive.

So what changed?

Why does half the world's population choose to live in cities now?

The story continues...

The **City** Surge

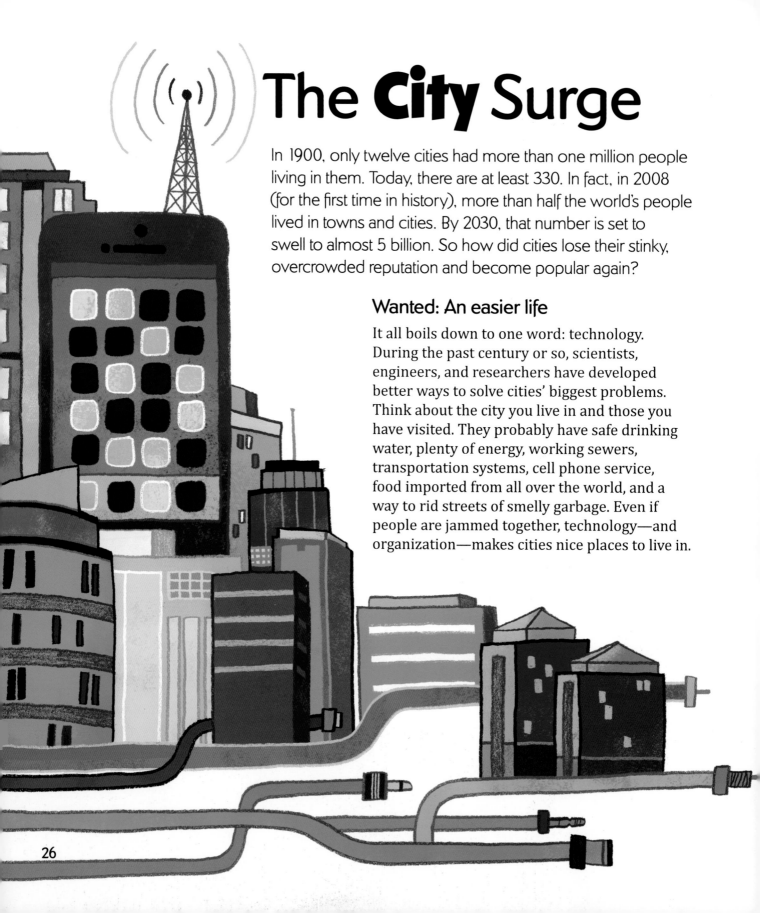

In 1900, only twelve cities had more than one million people living in them. Today, there are at least 330. In fact, in 2008 (for the first time in history), more than half the world's people lived in towns and cities. By 2030, that number is set to swell to almost 5 billion. So how did cities lose their stinky, overcrowded reputation and become popular again?

Wanted: An easier life

It all boils down to one word: technology. During the past century or so, scientists, engineers, and researchers have developed better ways to solve cities' biggest problems. Think about the city you live in and those you have visited. They probably have safe drinking water, plenty of energy, working sewers, transportation systems, cell phone service, food imported from all over the world, and a way to rid streets of smelly garbage. Even if people are jammed together, technology—and organization—makes cities nice places to live in.

Come together

Ultimately, people want to live in towns and cities because there's power in numbers. By working together and pooling resources and ideas, life becomes easier. Many hands make light work.

Generally, cities pull people because they offer...

- more and better jobs
- superior hospitals and medical facilities
- improved living standards
- more ways to socialize
- more choice for education
- cheap transportation

The countryside pushes people to cities because...

- the work doesn't always pay well
- in some areas of the world there's not enough easily accessible water or fuel outside of cities
- bad weather can make life hard for farmers
- there's less choice for education
- as more towns and suburbs are built, there's less land to farm

Population density matters

Why do some cities and towns feel more crowded than others? It comes down to something called population density — the number of people living in a certain area. Monaco in southern Europe is one of the world's most densely populated nations, with 36,000 people living in 0.75 mi.^{2} (2 km^2). (The entire country could fit within New York's Central Park!)

Not everyone would be happy living in such close quarters. A city of 100,000 people might seem HUGE to someone who enjoys living on a farm. But the same city might seem tiny to anyone from New York, the most populous city in the United States. Our opinion about what makes a place too crowded is more about our own likes and dislikes than population numbers written on a chart.

Live Where You Work

Jobs are a fact of life. And if you plan on sleeping in your own bed at night, you usually need to live somewhere near a job you can do. It's all part of how jobs help determine where people live.

Move to where the job is

People often move to be closer to where they want to work. And sometimes they move far. But did you know that companies consider where their employees might want to live, too? Some companies live by the motto "Build it and they will come." They start the business in a more remote location, betting that people will move there to work. Other businesses choose places where there are already lots of people living. These cities provide them with an instant workforce.

Small town or big city

The type of job you can do also has an impact on where you'll live. Take being a teacher, for example. For obvious reasons, you'll find schools in every city or town in the country. If your dad is a teacher, he can find work and live in all sorts of places. You could say this is a universal job, the kind you find near any place where people live.

But let's say your mom is a big boss at a bank. Her job is localized—that is, found only in specific areas. That means she must live where the bank's head office is. You'll usually find these buildings right downtown in large cities, not in small towns.

Heigh-ho, it's off to commute I go!

Transportation technology has come a long way, and it's a big reason why people can live a little farther away from their jobs. But the result of this technology? The commute.

The average commute time is about thirty minutes, no matter where you are in the world. That's a lot of time to spend getting to work. So why would anyone choose to live this way?

- As cities grow, more people want to live in areas close to their jobs. And they are willing to pay more to do so. Home prices downtown shoot up.

- As it becomes more expensive to buy or rent, some families move away. They find new homes that are more affordable by moving to smaller towns and suburbs (areas just outside the large cities).

- Now, however, people have a longer commute to get into work each day.

Gridlock—that's too many cars squeezed on roads—can also make commutes longer. Some cities are building better, faster trains to ease the load. Fewer people in their cars means less gridlock.

Not moving anywhere...

Thanks to cell phones, email, instant messaging, and computers, many people can set up a workspace nearly anywhere. Does it mean your dad can work for a Japanese company while living in Vancouver? Yes! Does your family need to live close to your mom's office downtown? Not if she works from home.

Because of the wonders of modern technology, people have way more flexibility when it comes to choosing where to live.

Live and learn

In 2012, commuters in London, UK, saved an average of $472,000 US on the price of their homes just by moving from downtown to a new place sixty minutes away by train. Their houses were bigger, too. These savings were enough to make some people choose to pack up and leave. Would you?

This Place Feels Just Right

You knew it the first time you spoke to your best friend: this person is amazing! You both love horses and know every player on your favorite baseball team, and you always have tons to talk about. This friend really seems to understand where you're coming from. You just click.

Guess what? The relationships we have with the places where we live are a lot like that, too. That's because a place's culture, available activities, and the attitudes of its people act like its personality. This personality plays a huge part in how connected many people feel to where they live. A lot of it comes down to what your city or town offers. For example...

➡️ **Love to kick a soccer ball?**

You'll be happiest living somewhere with fields and sports teams.

➡️ **Do you read a stack of books every weekend?**

Then you're probably going to want to live somewhere with a good library, bookstores, and kids you can start a book club with.

➡️ **Plan on being the next world-famous chef?**

City living with top restaurants on every street corner will make you feel most at home.

See? Different people need different things to make them love their community and want to stay. But a city's personality goes even further than that...

It helps us connect.

There's a reason people still head to the movie theater or sports complex, even though we can watch films and sports at home. Sitting together and laughing at a goofball on screen or cheering on the home team makes us feel like we're part of something bigger than ourselves. That's comforting and exciting. The same goes for hanging out with friends at the local park. It's fun!

Proof is in the personality

No one is saying it's a matter of life and death if we don't have culture, sports, parks, community centers, and libraries. It's not like they're water, shelter, or food, right? Maybe not. But when it comes to helping us decide where to live, a place's personality ranks right up there on the "Gotta Have It" meter.

Richard Florida—an expert on urban areas—wanted to know what gives a place its personality and makes it appealing. In other words, what do cities need to draw people to them? So he wrote down a question and sent it out to thousands of grown-ups in communities big and small as part of a survey:

"Why do you—especially if you have lots of choices—pick one place over another to live?"

The answers poured in and pointed to a few common things:

- A setting that mixes buildings with nature.

- A variety of people from many ethnicities, nationalities, and religions. Everybody feels welcome and anyone can fit in.

- Vibrant streets, restaurants, art, and music, and people enjoying the outdoors. It's a fun, busy, and exciting place!

Dr. Florida calls all this "quality of place." This welcoming feeling exists not just in big cities but in some smaller cities and towns, too. Maybe a town hosts a few fun festivals every year that draw people from all over. Or maybe it's located in a beautiful setting with access to rivers and hiking trails. It's just the kind of thing that might make you want to move there...and stay for good.

Planning a **Livable City**

Forget building little cities with Lego blocks. Some people have the coolest job on the planet — they actually dream up and plan real cities and towns. Their name? Urban (or city) planners. Their mission? To make places safe, organized, beautiful, and healthy so we can all lead better lives. If that sounds like a grand plan, that's because it is. Building livable space is also really important for a city's popularity. Remember: people generally move to cities to enjoy an easier, better life.

Welcome to Plan-o-ville

Good planning can equal better health, less stress, and more beautiful areas. You want to live there. Have a look.

Play ball! Sports bring people together

Tall buildings are spaced out

Plenty of schools

Easy-to-navigate grid system of streets

An exciting, busy downtown

Art and culture centers

Enough parking for everyone

From *oh no* to *ooh-la-la*!

Paris developed over centuries to become a confusing web of narrow medieval alleyways. That is, until city designer Georges-Eugène Haussmann entered the scene. Between 1853 and 1870, he knocked down entire city blocks and blasted wide roads through Paris. People thought he was crazy! But in the end he created the beautiful, open Paris streets people love to stroll down today.

New York, on the other hand, was quite a young city when it was designed with its famous grid plan. City streets run in straight lines, crisscrossing each other to make a net pattern. In addition, many streets are given numbers or letters as names so that you can "count" your way across the city. The plan was all about keeping order and giving people space, and it worked!

And don't forget Songdo, a brand-new city 20 mi. (32 km) from Seoul, South Korea. More than 25,000 people already live there and some are calling it the City of Tomorrow. It has a saltwater canal with water taxis, bike racks on each block, and garbage that shoots its way to the dump through pneumatic tubes. Neat!

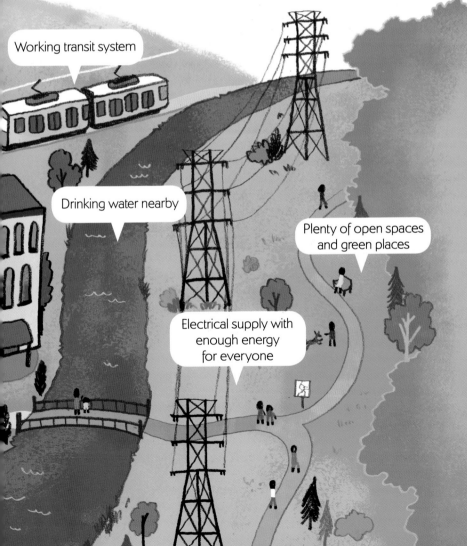

Working transit system

Drinking water nearby

Electrical supply with enough energy for everyone

Plenty of open spaces and green places

Too much of a good thing?

City planners first created suburbs to give families more green space and bigger homes than they could afford in the city. It was an urban-planning success story! But even great planning can lead to unintended consequences. For instance, suburbs created sprawl — when a city's outlying neighborhoods spread far from the core — making for long commutes and spreading city services thin. Now some city planners want to stop sprawl by getting more people to live in city centers again. But first they must ask: What new issues might pop up if they're successful?

Urban Planning Gone Wild!

What do you get when urban planners, architects, and engineers push themselves to the limit? Often the results are amazing livable spaces that put physics, nature, and, in some cases, good sense to the test. Let's take a look at some of the most extreme developments out there...

The height of cool living

Sure, there are high-rise apartments all around the world, but some new ones are taking life to the clouds. London's tallest building stands forty-nine storeys high. People who live in it report feeling it sway slightly during storms! But that's nothing compared to Dubai's Princess Tower at 101 stories. It has six basement floors just to hold all the residents' cars.

For sale: Waterfront

Dubai, a city-state in the United Arab Emirates, isn't just known for its mega-buildings. It's also home to artificial islands shaped like palm trees. They were built this way so that more homes—built along each "frond"—could enjoy a waterfront view. Workers have dredged tons of sand from the bottom of the Persian Gulf to create the islands, which are also set to hold luxury hotels, restaurants, shopping malls, and sports complexes.

Take a gamble on Las Vegas

Who in their right mind would build an entire city out in the desert? And not just any city, but one that houses a half million people and draws over 30 million vacationers a year to its casinos and mega-hotels! Tourists also flock to Las Vegas for attractions that include a fake Eiffel Tower, shark reefs, and indoor amusement parks...anything to draw a crowd. All that lighting and air conditioning requires so much power, it's estimated that Las Vegas uses more energy than Walt Disney World!

Welcome to Las Vegas! One of the most illogical places on Earth.

Troubled waters

The drive to strive and impress others is part of what makes us human. But when urban planners, architects, and engineers develop extreme buildings in extreme locations, the environmental impact of these projects is often no laughing matter.

For instance, in Las Vegas, tourists, fountains, and swimming pools suck water like a sponge. Yes, you can take three showers a day if you're vacationing there right now, but experts say Nevada is drinking itself dry: Lake Mead reservoir, the city's main source of water, is shrinking so fast, it could be gone in twenty years. Las Vegas is now looking for ways to pump water from hundreds of miles away, but it will cost billions of dollars.

So is extreme urban planning cool? Sure. These projects drive home just how creative and innovative humans can be. But as the water problem in Las Vegas shows, there is an important question we need to ask ourselves:

Even if we can build it, should we?

35

Life in the **Danger Zone**

Floods, fires, and tornadoes: not exactly what most people would put on their "Gotta Have It!" list when looking for a new home. But for some reason, whole towns and cities spring up in these kinds of risky danger zones. People who live there hardly give their location a second thought…until there's a disaster.

Pompeii pedestrians

It started with a rumble, then a roar, and then the city of Pompeii was covered by piles of ash. That was almost 2,000 years ago, but people are still talking about Vesuvius, the volcano that destroyed the ancient Italian city and killed thousands of citizens, who never saw it coming.

But here's something weird: over the centuries, people have moved back to this area, and not just a few—a whopping half million! That's an incredible number, since scientists say that the volcano will definitely erupt again. (It has erupted about three dozen times since 79 A.D., the year Pompeii was destroyed.) So it's not a matter of if Vesuvius will blow, but when…

Name your price

The Italian government knows it has a dangerous and deadly problem on its hands, so it's coming up with ways to get people out of the "red zone"—the area that will be hardest hit by an eruption. It established a national park at the top of the volcanic mountain so no one could build homes there. It has even offered cash to residents to get them to leave. Only a few thousand people have taken the money so far, though.

A view to die for

At first it might seem strange that people would choose to live close to an unstable volcano...not to mention a place where earthquakes, floods, or hurricanes are likely to hit. You would think we would all leave these areas and move someplace safer, right? But as the people living near Vesuvius show us, even money isn't always enough to get us to choose a new place to live. Why?

Advantages outweigh disadvantages

Put simply, in many areas where there is natural danger, there's also natural beauty. A volcano is dangerous, but its mountain is stunning. Oceans can bring tsunamis, hurricanes, and floods, but they also boast beaches and fun in the sun. Many of these danger areas also offer rich soil for farming, water for fishing, and a wealth of minerals such as tin, silver, gold, and copper.

Just risk it

Some people aren't all that bothered by risks and danger. Or they have a short memory. In January 2013, people on Hawaii Island started buying land destroyed by recent lava flows to build their houses. The land was cheap, so why not? They had the attitude that if another eruption happens, it happens.

Jobs and tourism

What makes areas dangerous also makes them fascinating. After Mount St. Helens in Washington State blew its top in 1980, way more people chose to visit the mountain. Because of this interest, hotels sprang up, restaurants and gas stations followed, and state parks were created. Soon, whole communities formed around these tourist-based job opportunities.

Because it's home

Many older civilizations developed in areas with volcanic or flooded soil because the earth was rich in nutrients and perfect for farming. Towns and cities grew in these places and became home to thousands and millions of people. When a settlement like this becomes so well established, we simply can't imagine that it wouldn't or shouldn't be there. It's home, despite all the dangers. So people stay.

Get Out of **Town**

There are many reasons why people leave or want to leave where they live. It's often because their town or city doesn't give them what they need: food, drinking water, safety, or the opportunities to build a good life. Take, for example, the tiny community of Batawa, Ontario. It started out as a large "company town" owned by Thomas J. Bata, a shoe tycoon who provided housing for his factory workers. The company built nearly everything for the village. But once the factory shut down, the citizens of Batawa had to move on, too.

There goes the neighborhood

In the U.S., Canada, and all around the world, dozens of towns and even cities go boom...and then bust. There's a rapid growth of work, money, and people before the whole economic system crashes. Sometimes the process happens quickly. Other times it takes decades for a place to die out.

Going...

Detroit. This American city has experienced a boom and bust. Parts of it are beautiful, busy, and full of life. But other areas are riddled with abandoned and rotting train stations, schools, hotels, and houses. Detroit was once a powerful center of the automobile industry and gave work to thousands. But many of the employees eventually moved to the suburbs, and jobs moved to other factories. Now Detroit is trying to come up with a plan to become a great city once again. Just a smaller one.

Anything but a ghost town

Some places you might think people would want to move away from are actually growing. Whether you call them slums, shantytowns, *favelas* (Brazil), *basti* (Bangladesh), *kampung* (Indonesia), or ghettos, many cities have these crowded areas marked by poverty and rundown houses. Many don't have access to schools, street lighting, or services to take care of clean water, sewage, and garbage. Today more than one billion people live in slums, either because they've come to try to make it in the big city, or because they have no other choice. Life in the country or along the coast has become too difficult.

When you don't have a home

At least families who move to slums have a roof over their heads. Many people who live in poverty—including kids—don't even have that. In 2012 in Washington State, there were nearly 27,000 homeless students living in shelters, motels, and even their cars. Thankfully more people are talking about kids who don't have a place to live—schools and agencies are stepping in to help, too. But a lot more still needs to be done to make sure everybody lives where they live because they want to be there.

Going...

Pripyat. This abandoned Ukrainian city used to be home to 50,000 people. Then, in 1986, the nearby Chernobyl nuclear power plant had a terrible accident and the government made everyone flee the city. Nearly everything was left behind—clothes, toys, TVs, and furniture. The area was poisoned by the plant's nuclear radiation. And yet, weirdly, several hundred people have returned to the area to live in the dangerous Exclusion Zone. Because no one can see deadly radiation, the risks don't seem real.

Gone.

Bodie. Peek through a window of a home in Bodie, California, and you might see broken kerosene lamps and chairs collecting dust. In the 1870s, Bodie was a busy gold-mining boomtown with nearly 8,000 people. But now? It's a museum. Don't even think of rearranging the furniture or swiping a rusty can as a souvenir. The people who preserve the place want to keep it looking exactly like what it is: a ghost town.

Climate Change on the Move

Scientists have been noticing something odd about our planet lately: it's getting warmer. This phenomenon is a type of climate change — which generally means any major changes in temperature, rain and snow, or wind patterns that happen over several decades or longer. But why is it happening? Could a changing planet change where you live?

Live and learn

How does climate change work? When people burn fossil fuels to power factories, homes, and vehicles, they add heat-trapping gases to the atmosphere. We call these greenhouse gases. As increased levels of greenhouse gases trap more heat in our atmosphere, the results can be surprising. They seem to be setting off all sorts of changes on land and in the oceans.

Who doesn't love a warm day?

You've got that right! Except global warming doesn't always lead to a balmy, sunny summer afternoon. Instead, we've got extreme weather all over the world: rains, droughts, and extreme heat and cold.

We see higher temperatures, of course. The decade from 2000 to 2009 was the warmest globally on record. Hurricanes are getting stronger, too, because they get their energy from warm ocean water.

Polar ice caps are also melting, and with all that extra water, oceans rise...with surprising effects. For example, higher water levels leave certain coral reefs and sea plants deeper under water— and without the sun they need. If they die, the fish that live there go hungry. If these fish go belly up or migrate, the people who fish them for a living might have to move, too.

H2-Whoa!

The truth is we don't know exactly how much the oceans will rise. But even 3 ft. (1 m) will make a huge difference to the millions of people who live within 60 mi. (100 km) of an ocean coast. Communities in Bangladesh, the Maldives, and Micronesia already struggle with rising water. High-tide seawater enters homes, floods cemeteries, and drenches farmland with salty water so food won't grow. People must move inland, often to city slums, to start a new life (see page 39).

Let's start now

We cannot predict what will happen one hundred, fifty, or even twenty years from now, but some places are already planning for the climate of the future. Take Chicago. It plans to build with new kinds of concrete, plant different trees, and grow plants on rooftops. Meanwhile, beach communities in places like North Carolina's Outer Banks, Cancun, and Miami are blowing sand from the bottom of the ocean onto eroding beaches to build them back up again and keep ocean water away from buildings.

Space, the Final Frontier

When seen from space, our planet looks like a shining marble sunk deep in the most velvety blackness you can imagine. It's hard to think of another place in the universe that seems so perfect. So *ours*. Yet some scientists say we should start thinking seriously about leaving Earth and living in space someday. Beyond fulfilling a basic desire to explore, why would we ever want to move? Especially if everything we need to survive is right here?

> "The nitrogen in our DNA, the calcium in our teeth, the iron in our blood, the carbon in our apple pies were made in the interiors of collapsing stars. We are made of star stuff."
>
> — Carl Sagan, astronomer

Reason no. 1

Earth may not be as suitable for life as it is right now. Climate change, a natural disaster, or extreme pollution could be the cause of trouble.

Reason no. 2

Many planets and asteroids are known to be full of metals and resources we could mine. In other words, countries might send people into space because there's money in it. Where there's profit, there are people who are willing to work for it and live nearby.

Reason no. 3

Although stars like our Sun burn brightly for millions, billions, or even trillions of years—eventually they all grow old and die. Knowing the Sun will no longer exist is an unsettling thought, right? But we're actually very lucky that stars become fiercely hot and blow up before they disappear. Other stars all over the universe have exploded in order to provide the material and energy to create planets just like our beautiful Earth and everything living here. Even you! But before our own Sun runs out of energy, we will need to find another place to live. Luckily we have billions of years to come up with a way to build space settlements.

5...4...3...2...1... Blast off!

Choosing the life of an intergalactic settler is easier said than done. At least for now. If we were to try it today, here are just a few problems we would face.

Far from perfect

Too hot, too cold, too far away, and no solid surface to land on. Most planets do not exist in a Goldilocks zone, or life zone. Our options for finding another perfect planet are limited.

They call it space for a reason

The universe is larger than most people can imagine. If you were to think of Earth as a grain of sand, you would have to travel 6 mi. (10 km) just to hit the next grain, Alpha Centauri, the nearest star system. Want to head to another planet even farther away? Using current technology, you would travel your whole life in a spaceship and never live to see your new home. In fact, your great-grandchildren and *their* great-grandchildren wouldn't either.

It's expensive

Space travel will need to be much cheaper if we're going to send thousands or millions of people into the wild black yonder. And don't forget the cost of building a colony. Who's going to pay for it?

Duck! Asteroids!

When he was living in the International Space Station in 2013, Canadian astronaut Chris Hadfield says he could hear small asteroids pinging off the walls, even though the station has armor. He wrote that he even watched a large meteorite burn up between the station and Australia. The thought of it hurtling toward him sent a shiver up his back. Yikes!

H2-uh-oh!

How do you grow enough food for people to eat if there's no soil? What do you do about water? How do you create gravity?

Home, home on the moon

There are still a lot of stellar reasons to reach for the stars and address today's challenges. Today astronauts are living for months at a time on the International Space Station high above our planet. They're learning all they can about life in space and sending back results. Many scientists believe that while we may not be ready to colonize yet, with enough excitement, creativity, money, drive, and time, we can find ways to adapt to space, too.

The **Happiest** Places on Earth

A laid-back vibe in St. Kitts. A totally kickin' soccer team in Barcelona, Spain. Political freedom in places like the United States, Canada, and Sweden. All these things make us happy that we live where we live. Psst! There's even better news. There are so many other ways to make your home even sweeter.

Is there a happiest place on Earth?

That all depends on whom you ask. These days a lot of organizations have been trying to figure out where the most content people live. Makes sense. If we know which communities and countries boast happy people, maybe we can all learn their secrets. One hitch: the data's all over the map—literally! Check out these "officially" ranked happiest places on Earth.

Be the change you want to see, and whether you live in a city, a town, or the country, your home will be the place you've always wanted.

World Happiness Report:
No. 1, Denmark

Why: political freedom, few government problems, good jobs, good health, and happy families

GfK Custom Research Report:
No. 1, Rio de Janeiro, Brazil

Why: good humor, good living, good festivals

Happy Planet Index:
No. 1, Costa Rica

Why: people live long, say they're happy, and the country cares about the environment

Hey, they can't all be number one. So which one is the best place to live?

Happiness. Get it in writing

Maybe remote Bhutan has got it right. In 1971 the country rejected the typical way to measure success and progress—gross domestic product. GDP measures the total dollar value of a country's goods and services produced during a specific period of time. Bhutan's leaders believe that being happy is more important than having money and things, so instead, they measure what they call gross national happiness! They aim to make Bhutan a friendlier, greener, healthier place to live. People there are now living twice as long as they did before the national change!

Make a happy place where you live

- Going for a hike with your family or friends? Bring a plastic bag or two and pick up any litter you spot along the way.

- Close off your street (just get the city's okay first) and have a neighborhood street party! Everybody brings a dish of food and enough plates for their family. Get to know your neighbors. Watch your street turn into a happier street.

- Is your local library in desperate need of a new building? Volunteer on its "friends of the library" committee to help raise funds.

- Set off fireworks with your neighborhood on holidays or head to where your city is lighting them. Be part of the crowd.

- Traffic is one of the biggest headaches for people living in cities. Make a pact with your family that you'll drive only if you absolutely need to. Otherwise, grab your bike or walk. It's a slower but happier way to start the day.

- Invite a friend over or keep in touch online. Isolation can make anybody sad.

- Make your neighborhood a friendlier place by offering to shovel snow or clean up the yard for older adults.

- Be a good neighbor. Pick up trash in front of your home, keep noise down, and be polite, and other people will follow the lead. Good vibes spread.

- Organize a school clean-up day.

- Learn another language so you can connect with a new culture in your community.

- Ask a local store if your class can paint a mural on one of its walls. Or approach city hall with your mural plan.

- Buy from your local stores when you can. You're keeping those shops hopping and making jobs.

- Play an instrument? Like to sing? Start a band and play for your friends.

- Plant a community garden and get to know the people in your neighborhood while you seed and weed.

- Take a walk. Get out and see the world.

Home: It's All Yours

Now you know all the outside forces and inner choices that have gone into why you live where you do today. Someday you're going to choose a neighborhood that makes sense to you. So what will you look for?

- ☐ Places to meet friends
- ☐ Yummy restaurants
- ☐ Near family
- ☐ A cool vibe
- ☐ The job of your dreams
- ☐ Clean water
- ☐ Convenient stores
- ☐ Wide-open fields
- ☐ Electricity
- ☐ A language you understand
- ☐ Historic buildings
- ☐ Friendly strangers
- ☐ Warm weather
- ☐ Honest politicians
- ☐ Feeling that you belong
- ☐ Something else?

Everybody's list is going to be a little different, and that's okay. Knowing where you want to live is a lot like knowing who you really are!

Glossary

Adapt
When people change or adjust what they do to suit the environment they live in so they can be safer and more comfortable.

Boomtown
A town that suddenly grows very quickly.

Citizenship
Being a member of a country or community. Citizens are allowed to vote but must pay taxes, too.

Community
A group of people who live together in a specific area. Sometimes they share a government.

Commute
To travel regularly between places, often between work and home.

Famine
A widespread crisis in which food is very scarce. People suffer from severe hunger and starvation.

Gross domestic product (GDP)
The value of goods and services a country produces. People often use it to measure a country's standard of living.

Immigrant
A person who moves to a country where she was not born so she can settle there permanently.

Industrial Revolution
A huge change that took place from the mid-1800s to the mid-1900s when some countries started focusing on manufacturing and technology instead of farming.

Nomad
Someone without a permanent home who roams from place to place, usually to find food.

Population
The number of people who live in a place. Populations grow and shrink as people move into an area or leave it.

Reservoir
A tank or lake used to store water for a community. It's sometimes used as a backup water supply.

Rural
The area located outside cities and towns.

Settlement
A new community that forms when people move to an uninhabited place. Every city and town started out as a settlement.

Shantytown
Sometimes known as a squatters' settlement or a slum. A town or a neighborhood within a town experiencing extreme poverty, where people build shacks or temporary houses to live in.

Suburbs
Communities outside of cities that are planned and developed to provide homes. They became popular places to live when city populations grew and transportation technology made it easy to quickly travel into the city for work.

Urban
Cities and city life.

Urban planning
Designing new and existing towns and cities so they are more enjoyable, organized, and safer to live in.

Index